HOW COMPANIES SAVE
MONEY BY USING
REFURBISHED
COMPUTERS

KEN CHAN

How To Take Advantage Of

Refurbished Computers

To Increase Productivity For
Your Company While Saving On
Operational Cost

This manual discusses refurbished
computers and how you can use them to
increase productivity for your company.
It gives you useful advices on what to
look out for when buying refurbished
computers.

CONTENTS

Every business needs computers to keep track of their expenditures, inventory and invoicing. At the same time, businessmen - especially start-ups with limited capital - are always looking for ways and means to reduce operational and overhead costs.

The technology industry is producing competitive features and trending designs at such a rate that it would be very costly for one to keep up with the latest gadgets and computer models.

So what should you do if you have a small budget but have a high-demand line of work? You have two options:

» buy a brand new computer that fits your budget but most probably will not be able to perform well; or

» get a refurbished computer with the right specs that will answer your needs.

Which would you rather go for? Refurbished of course!

If your keyboard or your monitor develops a fault or your terminal gets busted, don't go buying a full monitor-terminal-keyboard-package. Just buy refurbished computers or parts and you're settled.

Every responsible consumer would like to thoroughly check out the merchandise before they buy a laptop. They'd also check reviews online and if the company has any BBB unresolved complaints. The same is true with refurbished computers. However, "refurbished has given all the computers in this category the reputation of being defective. It sounds like a summary verdict without a trial.

What is Refurbished?

Refurbished computers are computers that were returned for reasons such as:

» the computer doesn't fit the owner's lifestyle, or

» the owner found a better one (remember returns are allowed for a limited time only so that technically means that the computers are still brand new).

Some other computers come under the category of being refurbished due to shipping damage like dents or scratches; or boxes were damaged. Some computers become refurbished when the original companies who bulk-leased them return them to the supplier after the lease contract expires. The suppliers then sell these computers as refurbished.

So as you can see, refurbished is not so bad after all.

Top Four Myths about Refurbished Computers You Should Ditch

Here are the top myths that are stopping you from getting the best value out of your money:

Myth Number 1:

Refurbished is synonymous with "damaged" or "fixer-upper"

That's not true. In truth, "refurbished" refers to computers that may have been reconditioned to its tip-top performance. It is not the same as "once damaged but is now OK", and doesn't mean that it has a shorter life-span than a brand-new computer because it has been used. Some refurbished computers haven't really been used. Some were demo computers or slightly damaged while in transit but has been fixed.

While brand new business computers would hurt a home user's wallet, refurbished computers allow home users to experience top quality performance without the costs.

MyTH NumBer 2:

Refurbished Computers Have Limited Warranties

All computers have an expiration to their warranties—and refurbished ones are no exemption to this. Before you bring home your machine, your store seller would let you know how long the warranty would be.

Refurbished stores would usually give add-on extended warranty, but this depends on the store you are dealing with. Be sure to read the fine print just to make sure.

MyTH NumBer 3:

Refurbished Computers Do Not Come with Licensed Software

When people think refurbished, they often see an image of a car stripped of all its insides and/or its paint. This is not the case with computers. Refurbished computers do come with licensed Windows software. Moreover, you can always check with your friendly refurbished store staff just to be on the safe side.

MyTH NumBer 4:

Refurbished Computers have Unfixable Bugs

The opposite is actually the case. Brand new computers are sold with 100% *perception* that everything is OK with them, but your refurbished computer had to be tested, retested and checked all over again before being put on sale.

Consequently, this means much care and rigorous testing is done focusing on individual refurbished machine to ensure that everything works with it.

You should always check out the condition of your refurbished computer. Buyers are well protected by warranties and guarantees so do not let any misconception stop you from using business class machines.

How Refurbished Computers Help Businesses Big and Small

Put More Money into Your Business

Buying refurbished computers allows you to pick only the parts that you need like maybe an external hard drive as back up. This saves you cost and allows you to put more money into your business rather than on expenses.

Keep in mind that refurbished computers are perfectly fine working machines that needed a software update or some parts changed to put it back on its tip-top shape. What's more, refurbished keeps business class hardware within your reach.

Budget-Friendly

Refurbished computers are sold ranging from half to a quarter of the price of a brand new model. Refurbished have the same warranties as your brand new ones. You can also ask your store to give you a help line in case you have problems setting up your computer.

Brand new computers usually have all these free software included that you don't really need? Well your refurbished computer won't have those but it will have the licensed core software needed to run it.

Help Save the Environment

Global warming is real. We have been following the news with humongous storms one after the other; traveling around the earth without care for borders or political differences. The aftermath is shocking too with hundreds to thousands of casualties when tallied together.

Computers are made to survive decay. So, when you buy a refurbished computer you are helping to save the Earth.

Combating the effects of global warming starts on a small-scale endeavor. It starts with a simple word: "me".

Reasons Why You Should Buy Business Laptops

Laptop makers differentiate between consumer laptops and business laptops, but it be beneficial to you if you buy a business laptop even if it's for personal use. Here are the reasons:

» Business-oriented products are made to survive abuse like drops and spills. So they last longer than the consumer laptops.

» They have better keyboards. This doesn't mean that the consumer keyboards are but let's look at Lenovo's ThinkPad keyboards. It has keys that are easy to feel without looking.

» Most business laptops have matte displays with better viewing angles even if they don't come with a touchscreen. Consumer laptop may have shiny displays, but the viewing angles may be really bad.

» Replaceable, Extended Batteries – you don't have to take them to the service center before you can remove them; unlike the sealed-in batteries.

» The prices are reasonable.

» They are more serviceable because their parts (batteries, AC Adapters and screens) remain in the market for years. This gives them longer durability.

» Most business laptops have biometric security.

Tax Cuts from Computer and Software Purchase

Section 179 is a piece of good news for all business owners and employees utilizing computers in their business or work. This includes software purchased for business purposes. So how does Section 179 really work? Here is a brief overview of how you can apply your computer purchase for your tax deduction.

What is Included?

Section 179 covers computers, software and refurbished computers (yes, refurbished too!) that are used for business purposes. If you are a business owner, you can deduct the full amount from your tax if you use the computers for sole business purposes.

Personal use can be deducted proportionally and excluded from the tax cut portion. Example, if you use your computer 30% of the time for personal use then instead of deducting the whole cost of your computer from your tax, you can deduct only 70%.

You can also check out a complete list of the qualified goods under Section 179 HERE.

What is Required?

The requirement for equipment to qualify as a business expense is that it should be used more than 50% of the time for business use. Quantify the cost multiplied by the percentage it is used for business to arrive at the tax deduction applicable.

The Limitations

The limitation set by Section 179 is at $2,500,000. Your total business equipment should not exceed the cap. If it does exceed, however, Section 179 provides deduction only up to that point. Also, you can't use Section 179 if your total expense exceeds your income for that year. This is true for start-ups. If it does happen, don't worry – you can save up the receipts and use it for future years when business profits start to turn in. Another way of utilizing Section 179 in case income is not so good is if you are filing joint tax with your spouse, then you can use your tax deduction under Section 179 when applicable.

How is it different from Bonus Depreciation?

One huge difference is that bonus depreciation is offered on and off. Sometimes, bonus depreciation is offered 100%! So pay attention and maximize such an opportunity to the fullest. Bonus depreciation is applied "after" Section 179. This is great news for large business owners whose expenses for equipment exceeds the cap set under Section 179.

Employees Can Use Section 179 too!

If you are an employee and you're using your own computer for your work more than 50% of the time then you can ask your boss to pay the proportionate amount and declare that as a business expense!

Unqualified? No Problem

In case your computer does not qualify for Section 179 because you use it less than 50% of the time for business or for work then you still have Depreciation to look forward to.

Tips When Buying Refurbished Computers for Business Use

When buying a computer for your business:

» Always consider the bigger picture. If your business would rely on computers then consider buying computers with the same parts and always pay special attention to your refurbisher's warranty, return and repair policy.

» Check your seller's reviews as well as service and return rates.

» Pay special attention to what is included in the warranty.

» If your refurbisher sells extended warranty, do well to get your machines covered. This will save you more money in the long run.

Where to Buy Great Laptops for a Steal

Ask a tech newbie what a great laptop is, and you may hear the latest trend and most hyped products; but if you ask a businessman what a great laptop is, you will hear specs ranging from old models, last month's model and their personal suggestions on what manufacturers can do better. So get the low-down from us on what a great laptop should look like.

  » It has great coverage in terms of warranty
  » Not the latest model but not the oldest one
  » Buy refurbished! They can save you a lot in terms of money.
  » Check out if you have the tech skills to handle the computer
  » Let the store know what you intend it for, as well as your budget so they can help find the best fit for you.

Why Buy Refurbished?

I know we keep on telling you this but you would have to know it when you've tried it. Refurbished computers are not fixer-uppers in a sense that the RFR (Reason for Return) is minor like people changed their mind or they feel like they can't live with the scratch on the surface of the laptop.

The refurbished computers you see on sale have been fixed and tested by experts.

Another source of refurbished machines is a corporate off-lease sale. Companies return the leased computers after three years and the store or company receiving the computers back would sell the machines for a much lower price. Just imagine all the big businesses in the area doing this.

Big companies understand that the fast rate of tech advancement means they have to update their computers in a short period of time therefore buying and owning computers is not a good investment in the long term. Regular people like us can then benefit from those three-year old machines. Not a bad deal considering that they are business class computers at a low price.

Finding a Good Store

Check online reviews and BBB profiles when thinking of buying a computer or laptop. Ask your friends or family for a referral too!

Here are some good sources for laptops:

- » Craigslist – you will have to read all the specs and warranty
- » Buy locally – you would want to be able to get tech support when needed
- » Ask friends or colleagues at work where they got theirs and how is it working for them so far
- » com – this app is a great help in finding local sellers!
- » Check out tech magazines or local newspaper ads

Save More With Us!

We at <u>The Mighty PC</u> offer great business grade computers at low prices. We provide great warranty coverage and tech support when needed. We also have an awesome referral program where you get discounts for referring a friend! Give us a call and let us know what you need – we can help you find the best computer for school, work or even for your business. Call us at 480-550-9078

About the Author

Ken is a serial entrepreneur and a Chinese-American Investor. With the enthusiast personalities, Ken strives for excellence in everything he does.

He found his company The Mighty PC and has helped countless entrepreneurs & businesses locally & nationally to secure over 200,000 (keep on growing) refurbished rebuild repurposed business computers. He provides companies with his computer knowledge and insight on how to increase productivity as well as cutting their operational costs at 30 to 60%.

He also co-found Future Kiddie, where he provides technology curriculum to preschools & learning center and teach young children computer skills to prepare for their future. As an educator, it is one of the many ways he gives back to the world and supports the community.

In addition, Ken is a lead generation expert with B2B and B2C experience. He co-founded the company High Ticket Solutions with a group of entrepreneurs and is dedicated in helping other business owners form strategic relationship with other entrepreneurs.

Furthermore, he is actively involved with forming different joint ventures with other entrepreneurs, blog on variety of business topics and seek for ways to give back to the society & support charity organization. He heavily invests himself with personal growth & development courses as well as investing with others in real estate or cash flow generation assets.

www.ingramcontent.com/pod-product-compliance
Lightning Source LLC
Chambersburg PA
CBHW031235050326
40689CB00009B/1618